the
WARRIOR
in
art

the
WARRIOR
in
art

By Nancy Forte, Designed by Wendell Carroll ■ Lerner Publications Company, Minneapolis, Minnesota.
Prepared under the supervision of Sharon Lerner, Art Editor

1362117

Detail, Battle Scene by Pieter Brueghel the Elder (1525/30-1569), Kunsthistoricshen Museums, Vienna.

Contents

Introduction   6

THE WARRIOR'S IMAGE

Warrior, Assyrian   8

Warrior, Etruscan   9

Battle of Darius and Alexander, Roman   10

Gemma Augustea, Roman   11

Charlemagne, French   12

Commander by Leonardo da Vinci   14

Equestrian Portrait of Emperor Maximilian
   by Hans Burgkmair   15

Officer of the Imperial Guard by Theodore Géricault   17

Napoleon in His Study by Jacques-Louis David   18

The Outpost by Jean-Louis Ernest Meissonier   19

Mato-Tope by Karl Bodmer   20

Warrior by Raphael Sanzio   22

Warrior by Conrad Marca-Relli   23

Knight-Errant by Oskar Kokoschka   24

Zapatistas by Jose Clemente Orozco   25

Portrait of a German Officer by Marsden Hartley   26

Artillerymen by Henri Rousseau   27

The Warrior by Henry Moore   28

General by Enrico Baj   29

Quote by Robert Rauschenberg   31

LEGENDARY WARRIORS

Hercules Wrestling the Cretan Bull, Greek   33

Theseus and the Minotaur by Jacques Lipchitz   34

David and Goliath by Marc Chagall   37

St. George and the Dragon, Russian   38

St. George and the Dragon
   by the Master of Brescia   40

THE WARRIOR'S PAGEANT

Study for Weapons by Leonardo da Vinci   41

Ramses II in His Chariot, Egyptian   42

Pursuit Scene from Nimrod, Assyrian   45

Bayeux Tapestry, French   46

Alexander Defeating Darius by Albrecht Altdorfer   49

Charge of the Light Brigade by William Simpson
    and Edward Walker   50

Rout at San Romano by Paolo Uccello   52 & 53

Battle of Constantine and Licincius
    by Peter Paul Rubens   54

Murat Defeating the Egyptian Army
    by Baron Antoine Jean Gros   55

The Battle of La Hogue by Benjamin West   56

Study for the Ammunition Wagon
    by Theodore Géricault   58

Defiance: Inviting a Shot by Winslow Homer   59

Guernica by Pablo Picasso   60

WHEN THE BATTLE IS OVER

Surrender at Breda by Diego Velazquez   62

Prisoners from the Front by Winslow Homer   63

Artillery by Roger de la Fresnaye   64

Eagle Warrior, Guatemalan   66

Gundestrup Caldron, Danish   67

THE WARRIOR'S GAMES

The Art of Jousting and Tilting by Leonard Beck   58

The Joust by Conrad Marca-Relli   69

The Combat of the Infantry by Jacques Callot   71

Chess Set by George Ortman   72

Introduction

From the earliest days, until the invention of photography, the artist was the camera of his age. He recorded events and the attitudes of people toward those events. This book will explore the history and image of the soldier and war through the eyes of the artist. We will see the various feelings of many different peoples and times toward war.

To find the first warrior we must return to the days before history was recorded. As civilizations developed the concept of the warrior differed. His weapons changed, so did his appearance, and, in turn, the artist's presentation of the warrior. And as men's ideas changed, so did the way artists depicted war. Once it was viewed as only a noble sport. Later painters stressed the suffering and destruction that have always accompanied warfare.

War has inspired men to heroism and cruelty. War has been both glorious and terrible. On the following pages we will see some of the different faces of war and warriors.

Some of the warriors we meet will be familiar. You will already know a great deal about them. Still others will be met for the first time. Each picture or sculpture represents the artist's idea of the qualities he sees in the real or imagined hero; the strength of Hercules, the goodness of David, the heroism of St. George, or the pride of Napoleon. Here are warriors as the artist depicts them in painting, sculpture, mosaic, collage and tapestry.

Cavalieri by Leonardo da Vinci (1452-1519); Galleria del' Accademia, Venice, Alinari-Art Reference Bureau.

The Warrior's Image

This one-man army is an Assyrian foot soldier of the early eighth century BC in the service of Sargon II, King of Assyria. The Assyrians were a war-like people who occupied the area which is present-day Iraq, Syria and Turkey. This warrior carries a bow, dagger, sword, and a club in his belt. He wears no armour. When you come to the Assyrian relief depicting a pursuit scene on page 45 you will see that this type of soldier does not go into the lines of battle. His job is to shoot arrows over the heads of the spear carriers and horsemen to protect them from attack.

Although the artist is interested in showing the warrior as realistically as possible, he walks in a very strange manner indeed. His legs, face and one arm are seen in profile, but his eyes, torso and the other arm are seen from the front. One reason for this awkward presentation was the desire of the artist to show as much of his subject as possible. This style of representation is found in Egyptian art, too. Either trade or wars could have brought Egyptian influence into the art of Assyria. Most interesting in this stone *relief,* or shallow carving, is the detail of the man's hair style. How fashions change! In their day, Assyrian men must have had to spend much time with their hairdressers.

A Warrior in the Royal Procession of Sargon (about 700 B.C.), Assyrian; Louvre, Paris, Alinari-Art Reference Bureau.

Armed and ready for battle, an Etruscan foot soldier stands holding his shield. The Etruscans are thought to have been a Greek tribe which migrated into northern Italy. This bronze soldier is only eight inches high and yet its unknown sculptor captures the detail of armour and helmet perfectly. The armour is made in sections of leather-like scales covered with bronze. The warrior wears no leg armour, because he depended upon speed for victory. Leg armour would slow his attack. His helmet, with its brush top and hinged side pieces, was an important part of his protective equipment. The helmet prevented direct blows to his head. The brush cushioned the strikes. The side pieces could flap down to protect parts of his face and neck. His shield helped to deflect arrows and sword points. In the now empty hand there was once a spear. The Etruscan fought at close range with simple weapons, so for his type of warfare he is well protected.

Warrior (about 300 B.C.) Etruscan; British Museum, London.

Alexander of Macedonia (355 BC-323 BC) was called Alexander the Great, a name we have all heard, but perhaps know little about. An artist, who lived about 200 years later, depicts here what he imagines must have been the face of this hero. With great skill the artist has made a realistic portrait of a young ruler, not with paint, but with colored stones. Such work is called a *mosaic.* Notice the detail in the armour's design. We can see that it is made in sections, most likely of leather decorated with bronze plaques and tied in place with cords. The face on the armour is of Medusa. According to Greek mythology Medusa was so frightening that anyone who looked at her was turned into stone.

This scene is only a portion of a large mosaic depicting the battle between Darius, King of the Persians, and Alexander. The battle was important because it marked the beginning of Alexander's advance to the western boundaries of India. His victories would make him, at the age of 32, master of the known world.

Alexander was an intelligent ruler who wished to bring Greek culture and government to the world. He was a brave and victorious warrior who was always at the head of his men in battle.

Detail from the Battle of Darius and Alexander at Issus (about 100 B.C.), Roman; National Museum, Naples, Alinari-Art Reference Bureau.

Warriors are proud of their victories and like to have the events remembered. Pharaohs, Emperors, and Kings had statues and monuments created to commemorate their conquests. The Roman Emperor Caesar Augustus (63 BC-14 AD) selected another way to honor his victory over the Germans. He had an artist carve his likeness on an onyx stone. Such a work is known as a commemorative cameo. Augustus is seated beside Roma, the representation of the spirit of Rome, in her warrior's garb. An unknown goddess places a crown on Augustus' head while Tiberius, his general, steps from a chariot. The Emperor is above the actual battle scene, surrounded by his personal symbols: the eagle, seagoat, and general's staff. His men are binding bearded German prisoners in preparation for taking them off to Rome. The detail and realism of this work make Roman art so different from the later Medieval portrait of Charlemagne.

Gemma Augustea (1st century B.C.), Roman; Kunsthistorischen Museums, Vienna.

Charlemagne (c. 740-814) upon his horse rides proudly, grandly on, forever. He does not look like a warrior, because this portrait shows him as ruler. In one hand is a sword, symbol of his role as protector, and in his other hand the orb, symbol of his rule of the Christian world.

What do we know of Charlemagne? He was a powerful king who fought in 52 campaigns. His conquests resulted in the creation of the Holy Roman Empire, of which Charlemagne was crowned Emperor on Christmas Day, 800 AD. You might think that such a successful warrior and ruler would have been an educated man, but history tells us that he could not write. He was a very tall man with a long nose, bright eyes, white hair, short neck, and a big stomach. His name was most apt, for in English Charlemagne means Grand Charles.

The rather rounded forms of the horse and Charlemagne all accent his big frame and heavy body. The detail found in earlier sculpture is missing here. This is a generalized portrait emphasizing only the subject's major qualities.

Charlemagne (9th century); Carnavalet Museum, France.

A Commander by Leonardo da Vinci (1452-1519); British Museum, London.

Leonardo da Vinci's commander is an unknown but proud and defiant warrior dressed in splendid armour. The visor of his helmet resembles the beak of some great eagle. Dragon wings, curling foliage and ribbons cover the helmet. A life-like lion's head snarls on the breastplate ready to eat the warrior's victims. What a spectacle to see a parade of such commanders in their dress armour of steel, gilded in gold and silver, catching the sunlight like a moving jewel box.

The armour of this period was polished and tooled like fine silverware. Artists like da Vinci were hired to design it for the wealthy rulers of Europe. The armour worn by kings was often so elaborate that it included plumes, ribbons, jeweled crowns, and velvet garments worn over the metal. These beautiful suits of armour were much too precious to be used in battle. They were like costumes, meant to be dazzling works of art. For real warfare less ornate armour was worn.

Equestrian Portrait of the Emperor Maximilian (1508) by Hans Burgkmair (1473-1531); The Cleveland Museum of Art, John L. Severance Fund.

Warfare and weapons changed a great deal from the time of the Etruscan warrior to the Emperor Maximilian I (1459-1519). Armour had become the most effective protection available against spear and lance attacks. It covered the entire body instead of only a small portion and was one of the most important parts of the warrior's equipment, valued because of its beauty and expense, as well as protective qualities.

A portrait of the Emperor in his armour turns into a portrait of the armour. Artist Hans Burgkmair who did this woodcut portrait also designed the Emperor's armour. As you can see, it is more than a protective suit of metal. A crown, peacock feathers, and cas-cading scrolls all decorate the helmet. Notice how the armour is hinged at each point where the body bends. It is no wonder that artists were involved in designing armour, for they would know more about the anatomy of the body than the metal craftsman. Also notice the curving of the armour. It does not follow the exact shape of the body. The curve was designed to help deflect arrows, clubs, and swords. Maximilian's horse also wears elaborate armour with a crown and crest to identify the animal as belonging to the Emperor. To carry the 150 additional pounds which the armour weighed, a heavy large-boned animal was required. He did not have to move quickly, but he did have to be strong. War in those days was slow moving.

Everything in this painting is tense and full of action as horse and rider shoot across the canvas like an arrow. The fiery spirit of the warrior and war horse as they charge through the smoke and dust of battle is captured by Theodore Géricault (zhay-ree-co) in his painting of a Napoleonic soldier. This warrior is no longer wearing the cumbersome armour of Maximilian's day. He again needs speed to attack the enemy, which now has guns and cannons. As these weapons came into use armour was discarded and the pace of war became faster. The warrior needed a sure-footed and swift animal, not the steady and heavy creature once used by the knights. Frenzy and excitement are expressed by this horse. Notice the way he springs into the charge, nostrils flaring, mane and tail whipped in the air. His speed is such that the soldier's jacket, plume and braid fly out into space as though a gust of wind has caught them. War is no longer slow and stately.

Officer of the Imperial Horse Guards (1812) by Theodore Géricault (1791-1824); Louvre, Paris, Alinari-Art Reference Bureau.

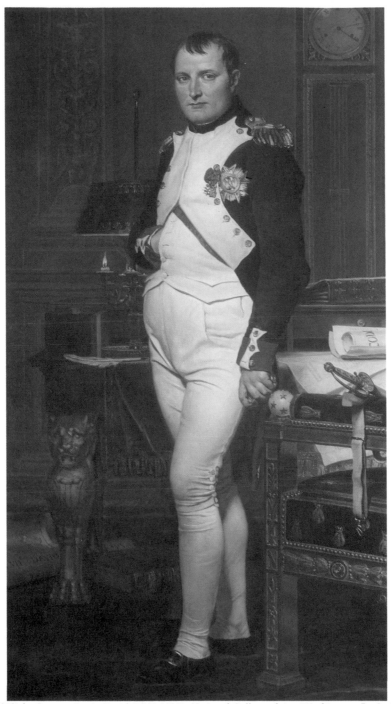

Napoleon in His Study (1812) by Jacques-Louis David (1748-1825); National Gallery of Art, Washington, D. C., Samuel H. Kress Collection.

Napoleon Bonaparte (1769-1821) was a soldier who rose to be the Emperor of France, although he was not of French birth. His homeland was the island of Corsica. In 1799, through his energy, ambition and military genius, Napoleon was able to seize power from the short lived democracy which followed the French Revolution and make himself Emperor.

Napoleon the general is portrayed by Jacques-Louis David (duh-veed), his official painter. It was David's job to portray his Emperor as a dynamic, powerful, stately and successful commander. We see Napoleon, posed in his office, dressed in his formal uniform and surrounded by the tools of his trade: maps, charts and military objects.

The Outpost (1880) by Jean-Louis Ernest Meissonier (1815-1891); Courtesy of The Art Institute of Chicago, A. A. Munger Collection.

Jean-Louis Ernest Meissonier is remembered for his historical paintings. He was fond of using soldiers as subjects. His military figures are rarely shown in combat, however. They are usually studies made from personal observation, for Meissonier would follow the troops of his day in order to paint from life.

The Outpost depicts a cavalryman on sentry duty, and is as much a portrait of the horse as of the soldier. There is no action, except a slight sense of watchfulness, as the soldier looks off into the distance. Perhaps his attention was attracted by some sound, for the horse, too, looks in the same direction.

The cavalryman is not alone in this picture. Very faintly in the distance there is the tiny image of another soldier. Can you find him?

Many of the stories we know about warriors come from the past and from Europe, but American Indians have also had a long warrior tradition. The tales of their battles were recorded on skins of animals rather than on canvas or stone, so through the years they have disappeared.

Fortunately, several adventurous artists traveled among Indian tribes and left us with pictures from actual Indian life. Karl Bodmer, a Swiss artist of the 19th century, painted this portrait of a Mandan Chief while on a trip through the West. The exact identity of the chief is unknown. It is thought to be Mato-Tope or Four Bears, who was a friend of Bodmer.

The chief poses proudly in his bright war paint and bonnet decorated with eagle feathers. He holds his tomahawk, ready to strike. The Plains Indians loved to use feathers, fringes and scalps as decoration on their war costumes, for while riding a fast moving horse these decorations streamed in the wind making a very dramatic sight.

Mato-Tope or Four Bears (1834) by Karl Bodmer (1809-1893);
Joslyn Art Museum, Omaha,
Northern Natural Gas Company Collection.

What do both of these works have in common? Look carefully and you can see the way in which a contemporary artist, Conrad Marca-Relli, and Raphael (RAH-fah-el), a Renaissance artist, use the same subject. Both capture the spirit of the warrior's movement with shapes which emphasize action, strength and the speed with which he strikes.

In Marca-Relli's painting we can see a very vague human form. The figure appears to be moving, changing, and turning. The shapes composing the figure are not like those in the background, which seem to be more solid. Marca-Relli's work does not show a figure. It is there, but hidden. The picture is a puzzle with many pieces to fit together before we can see the figure. In comparing, Raphael's warrior, like Marca-Relli's hidden one, moves violently. Raphael draws what he sees and knows of the anatomy of the body in action. Marca-Relli only hints at the structure of the body as it moves through space.

Warrior by Raphael Sanzio (1483-1520);
Galleria dell' arcid Carlo, Vienna, Photo Alinari.

Knight-Errant (1915) by Oskar Kokoschka (1886-   ); The Solomon R. Guggenheim Museum, New York.

For a 20th century artist to paint a picture of a knight is unusual, but Oskar Kokoschka (co-KOSH-ca) did. This is a *knight-errant,* or wandering knight, who traveled over Europe in the Middle Ages searching for adventure. At first sight the knight appears to be lying down, but looking closer we see that he is being carried by the wind, high in the air. Near him is a *Harpy,* a frightful creature from Greek mythology who snatched the souls of the dead. There is also a sleeping lion. The lion is usually the symbol of royalty or government.

Was this picture intended as a self-portrait of Kokoschka? It was painted before he left to serve in the army during World War I. He was like a knight-errant going out in search of adventure, but instead of going where he chose he was being carried to wherever the winds of war would choose to blow him. If he died, the Harpy stood ready to snatch his soul. The lion, who should rule, is asleep.

Kokoschka does not try to hide the brush strokes. They twist and swirl through the painting like a strong wind. The whole canvas reflects trouble and storm in a dark and mysterious world.

Zapatistas (1931) by Jose Clemente Orozco (1880-1949); Collection of The Museum of Modern Art, New York.

Zapatistas, the title of this painting, is derived from the name of the Mexican peasant leader Zapata, the mounted figure shown on the center-left side. Those whom he led were given the name "Zapatistas," which means "the followers of Zapata." They were landless peasants who revolted under Zapata's leadership in the hope of achieving reforms in that period of Mexican history known as the Revolution of 1910. This era was the final phase in the violent history of Mexico that began when she obtained her independence from Spain in 1821. In the first 100 years after independence it is said that approximately 100 revolutions occurred. Mexico was governed during that century by a succession of emperors, dictators, generals and presidents.

This long struggle for justice, economic progress and political liberty has furnished the subject matter for numerous paintings by the famous "big three" of modern Mexican art, Jose Clemente Orozco, Diego Rivera, and David Alfaro Sequeiros. Orozco (O-rose-co) is considered by many the greatest of this group. He was a painter, lithographer, and muralist. His most notable creations are murals, and he has covered the walls of numerous buildings in Mexico, and also the United States, with his work. They stress scenes of war, revolution, conquest, history, and the suffering of the common people.

Zapatistas is not a realistic picture. The artist's intention is to show his subject in an ideal light, because his sympathies were with these people and their cause. The design of the picture, with a band of marching peasants, grim faced and determined, followed by their wives, equally brave, conveys something heroic. Over the small band looms the great leader himself, as proud as the mountain behind him. These men are not warriors. They are *peons,* poor agricultural laborers, who have left their homes to fight, and now they carry rifles and machetes. The entire effect is striking. The sombreros and swarthy features instantly identify them as Mexicans. You might compare *Zapatistas* with *Washington Crossing the Delaware,* for both pictures tell a similar story.

Portrait of a German Officer (1914-1915) by Marsden Hartley (1877-1943); The Metropolitan Museum of Art, The Alfred Stieglitz Collection.

How would you start to make a portrait of a good friend? Some of us would choose to paint our friend at work, or with a favorite pet, or at a sport which he enjoys. We would want to show his likeness. But Marsden Hartley painted what we know as *Portrait of a German Officer* without showing us the man. This is not a portrait in the sense of being the picture of a person, but rather it is the spirit of one man as a military figure, his friend Karl von Freyburg who was killed in World War I. We feel in it the military tradition of Germany, with banners of ancient kingdoms, the Imperial flag, part of a spur, epaulettes, military badges, and the Iron Cross, a military decoration similar to our Purple Heart. In the left hand corner are the initials KvF, like a memorial plaque in a cemetery. It is a curious painting which shows no strong emotion at the death of a friend.

Artillerymen (c. 1895) by Henri Rousseau (1844-1910); Collection, Solomon R. Guggenheim Museum, New York.

Henri Rousseau (roo-so) captures the snapshot attitude, "let's take a picture," in his painting of 19th century French artillerymen posed around a cannon.

The soldiers' eyes stare intently out of flat faces attached to cardboard-like bodies. They are painted as clear-cut shapes standing out against the detailed and softly patterned background. In this painting, as in many others, Rousseau uses the design of the figures as a pattern for other shapes. The triangular shape of the figure arrangement is repeated in the shapes of the trees, the swords, guns and shadow in the foreground.

Rousseau was acquainted with military life, having served under Maxmillian, Emperor of Mexico. Unlike Géricault and Gros, he does not glorify the warrior. Does he give you an idea of what these soldiers are like? Can you tell what he feels about soldiers?

The public and many artists of his day felt that Rousseau was a poor painter, because he was self-taught and unskilled in drawing realistically. Pablo Picasso and Paul Gauguin, however, admired his work. They felt Rousseau's importance in changing the unimaginative painting style of their time.

The Warrior (1952) by Henry Moore (1894-   ); The Minneapolis Institute of Arts.

Neither Enrico Baj's (buy) *General* nor Henry Moore's *Warrior* are portraits. They are meant rather to express ideas or attitudes of the artist toward the subject of warriors. Neither of them show the glory of war.

This is not a victorious warrior. He is a man who is defeated. Moore expresses the spirit of the wounded soldier still defending himself with his only remaining weapon, a shield.

He cannot see for his eyes are only holes in a head which has been cut open. His mouth is sewn shut. He cannot speak. His arms and legs must have been strong, but now they are gone. He is helpless. Here is not the unconquerable hero like Hercules. This is the not yet dead, but already hopelessly defeated, warrior of all history. Even the sculpture looks old, as if it were damaged by time, yet it was made only about 13 years ago.

General (1961) by Enrico Baj (1925-   ); Galleria Schwarz, Milan.

A warrior or wild man? Enrico Baj doesn't see strong, brave qualities in the soldier. His *General* is a screaming monster with dog-like teeth, blank staring eyes, a blood caked and medal encrusted uniform, jumping up and down in an insane tantrum. Other artists like Winslow Homer, whose work we will see, paint war as they observe it without comment. This is Baj's portrait of the Fascists who brought disaster to his country, Italy. It is also a warning against militarism.

Artists of the 20th century have been very critical of soldiers and war, because war today means the destruction of thousands and thousands of people. War is no longer a spectacle of knights on horseback riding against other knights on a battlefield. Soldiers who fight the war, and women and children who do not, are killed. To Baj war is destruction under the direction of monster generals. He has created a series of these inhuman creatures in the form of *collages,* or works of art made from bits and pieces of cloth, hair, clock faces and medals.

One of our modern warriors parachutes through space amid photographs of the late President Kennedy, boxes, and warning signs. He is not in battle against any human enemy. His struggle is to conquer the forces of outer space. The enemies which this warrior encounters are invisible: lack of air and gravity, destructive rays, and extreme cold. He must be protected against these, just as knights were protected, by wearing armour. Modern armour is also silvery and shiny, but it weighs only ounces and allows the wearer to move freely in his weightless world. The astronaut is only part of the painting, for this work is not a portrait. It is an artist's view of our world today. The newspaper photographs show the news of the day and the people who make the news, like the President. The warning signs might represent those people who warn us not to explore space, for it holds great dangers. The meaning of the painting is not entirely clear. This contemporary artist asks us to fit his images together and find our own meanings in the work.

Quote (1964) by Robert Rauschenberg (1925-   );
Collection of the Artist.

Legendary Warriors

Legendary warriors are often pure inventions, but some have their origins in history. These warriors have special significance in the minds of men. We remember the great Greek heroes Hercules and Theseus, the Israelite David and the Christian warrior-saint St. George. They were frequently chosen as subjects for paintings, sculpture, and other art forms.

The mighty Hercules, one of the favorite Greek heroes, known for his monumental strength and terrible temper, is seen wrestling with the Cretan bull. This is no game he plays, but rather punishment for a crime. Hercules, in a fit of madness, killed his wife and children. To be forgiven for this horrible deed he had to perform 12 almost impossible tasks. When he had successfully completed these labors he was pardoned. One of his great tasks was to capture the feared Cretan bull.

Vase painting was considered a fine art in ancient Greece and legends, such as the *Labors of Hercules,* were frequent subjects for these paintings. As early as the sixth century BC painters signed these vases. They took pride in their work and it was highly valued by the Greek people. Vases were collected by Greeks in much the same way as people collect paintings today.

This vase painter makes Hercules and the bull look like shadow puppets cut from paper: heavy black shapes with little detail. Although Greek artists were known for their skill in depicting movement and portraying figures, they were equally skilled in using only simple lines to capture the spirit and express an idea.

Hercules Wrestling the Cretan Bull (6th century B.C.), Greek; Walker Art Center, Minneapolis.

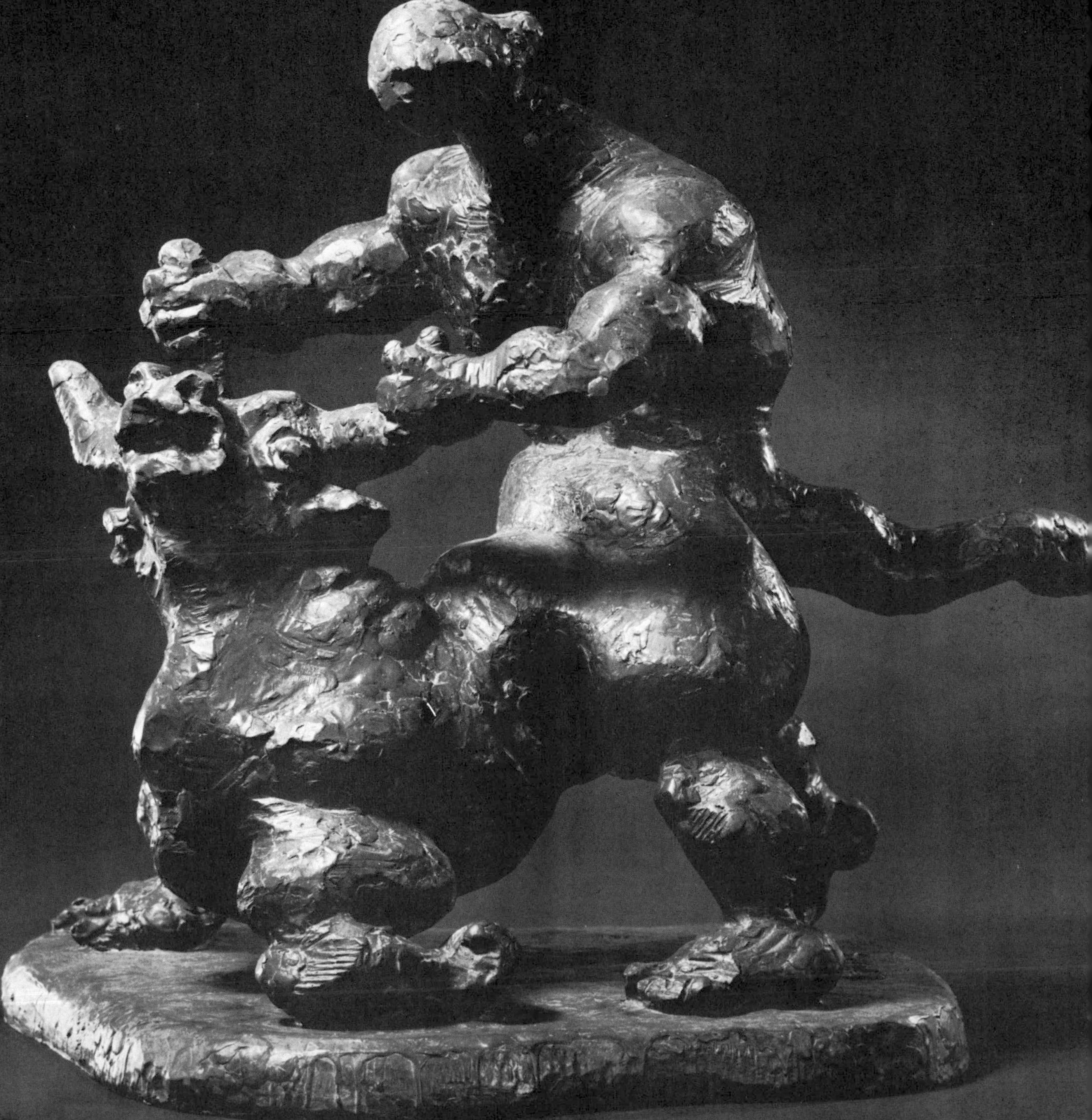

Theseus and the Minotaur (1942) by Jacques Lipchitz (1891-   ); Walker Art Center, Minneapolis.

Sculptor Jacques Lipchitz retells the ancient Greek myth of Theseus, Prince of Athens, and his victory over the monstrous half-man, half-beast called a Minotaur. Theseus had been sent as one of seven young men to be eaten by the Minotaur. But instead he killed the monster with a sword.

The sculpture shows Theseus plunging the sword into the Minotaur and twisting his head backward. The creature falls dying. Large bulging and rippling forms emphasize the struggle for life between these two powerful creatures. As exciting as this sculpture is to see, Lipchitz meant to do more than just retell a legend. The figures are not realistic. He does not give Theseus a face. Yet the Minotaur opens an almost human mouth to scream, and the two creatures share the same legs. Has the artist changed the man into a beast and the beast into a man? Perhaps he is telling us that man is really only fighting the evil in himself.

1362117

Lipchitz expresses the same quality seen on the vase, that of the monumental strength of man and beast. He goes further than the vase painter for he adds emotion. Lipchitz also has the advantage of being able to make round forms in space. The vase painter must make his subject conform to the shape of the vase. Hercules' encounter with the bull is a flat pattern. But both have the common idea of combat, with figures joined together, emphasizing strength and tension in locking forms.

David and Goliath (1931-39)
by Marc Chagall (1887-   ); Private Collection.

A shepherd? A soldier? A king? Think for a minute and you will know this young warrior. He is David, whose life is told in the *Old Testament.* The most famous story about David is his encounter with Goliath, which the present day artist Marc Chagall (shah-GAHL) illustrates here in an *etching.* Etchings are made by burning an image with acid on a copper plate. The plate is then inked and run through a press, making it possible to produce many copies of a single drawing.

David is not presented as a warrior. He wears no armour. He does not look like a fighter. Even as he holds Goliath's head he seems to be gentle; perhaps puzzled at what he has done. Chagall does not choose to picture David as he hurls the stone. This is not a man who is known for his strength. David is seen as a thoughtful person, not violent or even strong.

Look again at Theseus. How does the artist make him appear strong? Both are the work of modern artists, based on stories from the past, yet both are different. Each artist selects the outstanding qualities of his subject and exaggerates them, so that we see the strength of Theseus and the gentleness of David.

St. George and the Dragon (15th century), Russian; Tretyakov Museum, Moscow.

Like Theseus and David, St. George was a real person. He was born in the third century AD in the Roman province of Cappadocia (in the area of Turkey) and was a Roman soldier who was converted to Christianity. He was later beheaded for converting others to his faith. The dragon, his traditional foe, did not really exist, but was symbolic of evil, the devil or the plague. In the churches of Greece, Russia and Bulgaria you will find many paintings which resemble the picture from Russia of St. George slaying the dragon. As you can tell, it is not a portrait. The flat shapes, the curving forms of the body of horse and rider, the hand of God extending through the cloud and the delicate, feathery dragon are not meant to represent real beings. This is a style of painting developed by the church to remind the worshipper of a saint and his works. It is called an *icon,* which in Greek simply means image.

As heroic as the real life of St. George was, it is the legend about St. George and how he slew a dragon that is best known. The legend may have grown out of the attempt to explain an icon picturing St. George, the dragon and a maiden. The dragon is a symbol of evil and it is thought that the maiden was a representation of the province of Cappadocia (just as Uncle Sam stands for the United States).

Another story tells that near the town of Selena in Lydia (also part of Turkey) there lived a dragon, who made his home in a swamp. In order to prevent the dragon from killing them, the townspeople fed him their precious cattle. However, after many years the supply was exhausted and another form of offering had to be found. It was decided to draw lots and sacrifice the unlucky person whose name was drawn. The unhappy choice fell on the princess Cleodolinda. Dressed in her finest clothes, she was taken to the swamp. St. George, a Christian knight-errant, rode by and saw her danger. Calling on God to help, he charged the dragon and slew him with a spear. The princess, and the town, were saved. All were so grateful they converted to Christianity. St. George then left them to continue on his journey to the Holy Land, and to his death.

St. George and the Dragon (15th century) by the Master of Brescia, Italian; Photo courtesy of the Civic Cultural Institute of Brescia.

The St. George legend was a favorite subject for painters of the 14th and 15th centuries. It gave the artist a chance to dress St. George in beautiful armour and picture the princess in her royal attire. A 15th century artist created the second St. George painting of a handsome, young knight in his splendid armour, decorated with gold ornaments. He is riding an equally beautifully decorated horse, while a dragon coils ready to strike. The princess stands quietly by looking regal and fashionable. The figures are from the story, but the buildings are probably from a town in northern Italy. The painter very skillfully blends fact and fantasy, as does the legend itself.

To the people of the Middle Ages, St. George was the model of a knight-errant of the church. He served as patron saint of England, the towns of Venice and Ferrara in Italy and the guild of armour-makers.

The Warrior's Pageant

Battles are the offices or workshops of warriors. This is where they work, using all the skill and training they possess to win the battle. The gathering of troops, parades, and battle scenes are all part of the subject which artists have found exciting, terrifying, or hateful—war.

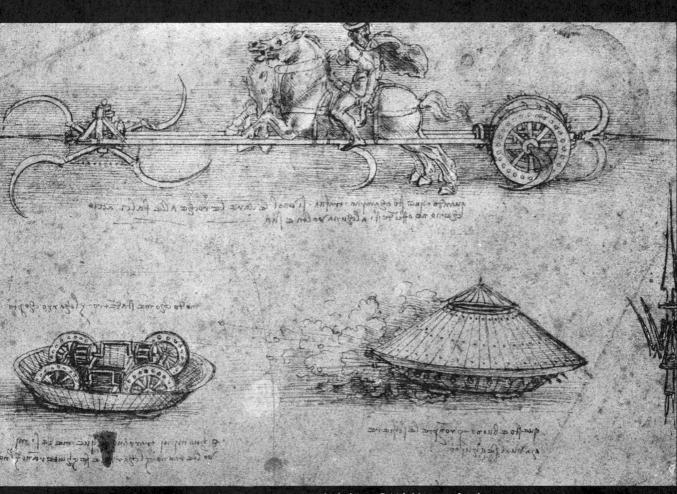

Study for Weapons by Leonardo da Vinci; British Museum, London.

Today our weapons are the most terrible possible. Yet, probably, these sketches from Leonardo da Vinci's notebook seemed as terrifying to the men of his time. Da Vinci is best known today as a painter, but he once earned his living as the Duke of Milan's war engineer. The sketches represent ideas for offensive weapons. The giant-sized scythe powered by horses cut through the enemy ranks, chopping everything in sight. In order to prevent damage to the Duke's troops, there was a mechanism to raise the blades while in friendly territory.

The other strange looking machine is da Vinci's version of a tank. It was powered by men turning cranks which moved the wheels. Made of wood and steel, it had revolving cannons and a look-out platform. Although it is a design from the 15th century the sketch looks a great deal like the Civil War ship the *Monitor*.

Ramses II in his Chariot (1292-1225 B.C.); Temple of Abu Simbel, Egypt.

Leaping horses pull the king in his chariot toward his enemies. He stands alert, ready to send the fatal arrow into the target. Pharaoh Ramses II (1324-1258 BC) commissioned this work to illustrate his skill as a warrior. We can see that this is not a specific portrait. We do not know what battle is being fought. Ramses and his chariot driver are the only people drawing their bows. The men at one side of the stone *relief* are much smaller than the king and are not participating in the fight. The horses look flat and are frozen into an unnatural position. The artist's intent is to show the king as a hero, saving his troops singlehandedly. The awkward position of the figures was the usual way Egyptian artists represented figures. They knew that the human body did not move or look this way but they wanted to show as much of their subject as they could. Egyptian artists also felt that such rigid movements lent dignity to the ruler and set him apart from common men.

This relief comes from the temple of Abu Simbel, built by Ramses II for his own glorification.

Pursuit Scene from Nimrod (about 650 B.C.);
Louvre, Paris, Alinari-Art Reference Bureau.

What an impressive sight this battle must have been. There were thousands of foot soldiers and horsemen, accompanied by musicians to stir them on. Paintings and sculpture give us some of our most detailed accounts of such ancient warfare.

This is only a small portion of a *frieze* (frees) which covered the walls of an Assyrian palace in the seventh century BC. The frieze was intended to illustrate the greatness of King Assurbanipal and his army, and serves the same function as the *Bayeux* (by-yuh) *Tapestry* on the next page. Most Assyrians couldn't read, and Assurbanipal, wanting them to know of his strength, had to select a way to inform his people. Pictures were the solution. Because the relief reads like a cartoon-strip it was necessary to walk around the palace several times in order to see all the battles in correct order. The top portion of the segment here tells of the gathering of the troops, and shows foot soldiers carrying their weapons, walking in single file and clapping hands in rhythm to the music performed by the musicians below. The lower portion shows various soldiers. Some are on horses, others are spearmen and archers. There are similarities in the way the Egyptians and Assyrians pictured people and animals. Can you find them?

Fragment of the Bayeux Tapestry (11th century); French Embassy Press and Information Division, New York.

This is only a small fragment of the *Bayeux Tapestry*, a huge work over 200 feet long that is named for the French town where it now hangs in the cathedral.

The subject is the conquest of England by William the Conqueror (1027-1087). The section shown here is a gathering in the palace of William's generals, and two charging warriors. The figures are embroidered in bright colored yarns on off-white cloth. They are small and almost delicate, like children's drawings. The warriors do not seem ferocious or strong like Theseus or Hercules. Unlike most portraits of warriors, this one was created by a group of women, William's wife, Queen Matilda, and her ladies-in-waiting. They were not trained as artists and did not have an artist's skill in drawing figures and yet the tapestry is beautifully made and of great interest because of the freedom with which the story is told.

The entire tapestry relates the events and battles which led up to the invasion and final victory of William at Hastings. Its purpose was to tell the story in such a way that even those who could not read would understand. For that reason, each part of the story is carefully detailed. The borders of the tapestry depict stories of knights and illustrate folktales.

*Alexander Defeating Darius (1529) by Albrecht Altdorfer
(1480-1538); Alte Pinakothek, Munich.*

Albrecht Altdorfer skillfully captures the excitement of battle through the churning masses of horses and warriors, pushing and pulling against one another. Above we see Nature's own conflict, as clouds roll and twist in stormy circles around the sun and moon. The picture is presented in much the way a movie producer would direct a mass battle scene. The artist gives us a huge view of thousands of people struggling in combat. The painting is so overwhelming in detail that we are almost unaware of the major figures, Alexander and Darius. The mosaic on page 10 is a scene from the same battle. You must look very closely to find Alexander, with spear lowered, charging the retreating Darius in his chariot. As you study the work, details which seemed to be right at first now seem strange. Isn't it odd that these early Greek warriors look like knights of the 16th century? Altdorfer lived during that century and this battle is a good example of the warfare of his day. There was great interest then in all aspects of ancient Greece. Greek writings were rediscovered and published. Altdorfer read actual accounts of the battle. He wanted his painting to be historically accurate. His research led to interesting detail such as the battle formation called the "Hedgehog," which was used by the Greeks and, much later, by the troops of Altdorfer's day. See if you can spot groups of foot soldiers with spears and shields bristling like a pincushion.

ALEXANDER M DARIVM VLT: SVPERAT
CA SISIN ACIE PERSAR: PEDIT: C.M. EQVIT
VERO X M INTERFECTIS. MATRE QVOQVE
CONIVGE. LIBERIS DARII REG:CVM M HAVD
AMPLIVS EQVITIB: FVGA DILAPSI. CAPTIS.

*Charge of the Light Brigade (1854) by William Simpson
and Edward Walker; Parker Gallery, London.*

Three perfect rows of charging horses speed across the battlefield toward the cannons while reserve troops of the opposing forces stand ready to charge. How different in feeling is this scene by Simpson and Walker from Altdorfer's. We see order and plan here, disorder and chaos in the other. Simpson and Walker's work objectively presents the facts. Altdorfer overwhelms and draws you into the fever of battle.

What a splendid scene! Here are two sections of a painting done in three parts. It looks more like a stage set than a real battle. Notice the beautiful armour. Knights on ornamented horses are placed in battle position. Even these realistic details, however, do not make the scene look alive, for the men and horses are stiff, as though carved from wood. They seem to be puppets. The artist, Paolo Uccello (you-chell-o), is not so interested in showing the battle as he is in using the newly developed tool of *perspective* to create the illusion of space, and making a flat surface appear to have depth. Notice how the fallen knight and all the broken lances on the next page point to a common spot. Our eyes naturally follow the lines like a directional arrow to the top of the picture. These devices fool us into believing that the flat canvas really has depth, an important tool in landscape painting.

Uccello was a pioneer in painting battle scenes. Cosmo de 'Medici (1389-1464), a ruler of Renaissance Florence, commissioned these pictures of the de 'Medici victory at San Romano, where a surprise attack of Sienese troops in June of 1432 was repelled. The paintings emphasize the victory of the de 'Medici troops over the attackers after an eight hour struggle. The man on the white horse is Niccolo Maurice da Tolentino, leader of the victorious de 'Medici troops. The other leader is Micheletto da Cotignola, who brought reinforcements. A beautiful and impressive painting, it was meant to show the strength and power of the de 'Medicis.

Rout at San Romano (1432) by Paolo Uccello; Louvre, Paris, Alinari-Art Reference Bureau.

Rout at San Romano (1432) by Paolo Uccello: National Gallery, London.

There are few war scenes in which so much action takes place as in this painting by Peter Paul Rubens. The artist makes us feel the excitement of battle. Cloaks fly, and manes and tails whirl as if whipped by the wind. Soldiers are seen at the moment of battle with swords drawn, beating off attackers and trampling over the dead and dying. Even the figures of Constantine (272-337) and Licincius push and butt against one another, urging their horses forward into the thick of battle.

But what does a battle from early Christian times have to do with 17th century France? Louis XIII (1601-1643), King of France, a Catholic, was struggling with a group of Protestants, the Huguenots. He felt that, like Constantine Emperor of Rome, he was waging war with the pagans and would be victorious. Rubens was commissioned to make a series of sketches based on Constantine's life. These sketches were to be used as the basis for a series of tapestries. What we admire as a great painting was only a sketch for another popular art form in 17th century France.

Battle of Constantine and Licincius (1622) by Peter Paul Rubens (1577-1640); William Rockhill Nelson Gallery of Art, Kansas City.

Baron Antoine Jean Gros (grow) loved the chaos and turmoil of war. His paintings are based on his own observations during battle, so they capture the immediate quality of action, much like photographs.

In this painting Murat, a general in Napoleon's army, is the central figure on the white horse. He leads his cavalry over the bodies of the defeated Egyptians, slashing anything in his path. The dashing figures of the horsemen seem to push the Egyptians out of the painting.

Baron Gros was a member of Napoleon's staff. His job was to select paintings from captive nations to be included in the Louvre collection and to paint records of successful campaigns. Napoleon considered painting a valuable form of propaganda, as have other military leaders of the past.

Detail, Murat Defeating the Egyptian Army at Aboukir (1808) by Baron Antoine Jean Gros (1771-1836); Courtesy of the Detroit Institute of Arts.

The Battle of La Hogue by Benjamin West (1738-1820); National Gallery of Art, Washington, D. C., Mellon Collection.

When we think of war, we usually recall land battles, but important fights have taken place at sea, too. Benjamin West, an American artist who lived most of his life in England, records a furious battle between the French and English off the Cape of La Hogue in 1692. With this victory the British repelled France's plans for an invasion of England.

This battle took place almost 40 years before West was born, but through written accounts and a vivid imagination, West has recreated his own version of the thick of the fight, as wounded men drown above slashing swords and smoking ships.

Even though paintings of battle scenes seem most exciting and tales of famous warriors the most interesting, Theodore Géricault (zhay-ree-co) preferred the ordinary soldier of his day as a subject. Strangely enough, the soldier is seen in defeat not victory. Géricault sketched his subject at the height of battle, straddling an ammunition wagon, grasping a lighted fuse and defying the enemy to come closer. He shakes his fist in anger as the battle rages around him. He is caught up in his own private war. This is a final gesture of bravery. In this action the artist sees the spirit of a proud but defeated France which would go down fighting.

Study for The Ammunition Wagon (1818) by Theodore Géricault (1791-1824);
Courtesy of The Art Institute of Chicago, Tiffany and Margaret Blake Collection.

A lone figure silhouetted against a light sky dares the enemy to shoot. In Géricault's sketch we find the same spirit. Here an American Civil War soldier shakes his fist at his enemy. He stands atop the barricades shouting at the soldiers across the field, while a minstrel plays songs to entertain the troops. In the distance, puffs of smoke remind us that this is a battlefield where fighting will soon resume. The battle scenes of Uccello and Altdorfer are about warriors, but we never sense fear or anger in their men. Winslow Homer captures these feelings in this young soldier issuing his challenge to fight.

Defiance: Inviting a Shot Before Petersburg, Virginia (1864) by Winslow Homer (1836-1910); Courtesy of the Detroit Institute of Arts.

The warrior is not so evident in this painting by Pablo Picasso, for it is really a painting about the horrors of war.

A dying horse opens its mouth with a terrifying cry. Heads and bodies are everywhere. A woman thrusts a lighted lamp from the window as if to see what has happened. Everything is confused and jumbled. Where is the warrior? Only the broken sword, a head and an arm are evident to hint at the warrior's fate. This is the truth of war. Picasso squeezes and pulls faces and bodies out of shape. The arms which stretch out of small bodies have grasping hands which express pain and fear. The horse screams as it dies. Its mouth is stretched open as far as it can go and its tongue is like a sharp knife. Its head is twisted with pain as its cries shatter the town.

The picture is painted in only white, grey and black. To Picasso war was not colorful. *Guernica* was painted to express his horror at hearing of the total destruction of this town during the Spanish Civil War. Another great Spanish artist who has also expressed his hatred of war is Francisco Goya (go-yah).

Guernica (1937) by Pablo Picasso (1881-   ); On Extended Loan to the Museum of Modern Art, New York, From the Artist, M. Picasso.

Detail from Guernica, top right corner.

When The Battle Is Over

The moment all warriors fight for and want most is victory. Both sides feel they will win, but each knows they may not. For the victor there is celebration. For the loser there is sadness and waiting, wondering what the victors will do.

Surrender at Breda (1634-35) by Diego Velazquez (1599-1660); The Prado, Madrid.

These men greet one another as though they were friends, but are they? The title tells us that this picture is the surrender of a town, Breda in Holland, to the Spanish leader Ambrigio di Spinola. High on a hill overlooking the battlefield, Spinola receives the key to the city from the Dutch leader.

How does the artist tell the surrender story? The Dutch troops stand at the left with heads hung down. Their spears are resting on the ground. Notice how tired and discouraged they seem. Their leader bends and leans toward Spinola, almost as though he has just knelt before the victor. The Spanish troops stand observing. Their spears are held erect, their armour is polished and they look alert and pleased. They had fought hard for victory and the battle had been a long one. Through the expressions on the men's faces and the way in which they stand the artist tells the story of the end of a battle.

Prisoners from the Front (1866) by Winslow Homer (1836-1910); The Metropolitan Museum of Art, Gift of Mrs. Frank B. Porter.

Notice how the two soldiers look at one another. You can see at a glance they are enemies. The Confederate soldier stands with his hand on his hip staring at the Union commander, daring him to ask questions. Homer very accurately conveys the attitudes of prisoners. They don't know what their fate may be, but they seemingly don't care. Except for the defiant soldier, we might mistake these three people for tramps. Their uniforms and appearance give us no idea that they belong to an organized army. In contrast, the Union soldiers are well dressed and orderly. We see the Confederate army before its final defeat—tired, tattered, and ready to surrender. Winslow Homer used sketches, which he made as a Civil War correspondent for *Harper's Magazine,* as the basis for many paintings. He is also known for his paintings of the sea.

Artillery (1914-17) by Roger de la Fresnaye (1885-1925);
Collection of Mrs. Wolfang Schoenborn, New York.

We do not feel great speed here. The soldiers are not in battle. They are on parade, perhaps a victory parade. As drums roll and trumpets blare, the soldiers march down the street. The artillery gun appears to be the most important part of this painting, but it is not painted realistically. The artist has reduced it to circles and rectangles. Looking carefully at the rest of the painting you will see that all the figures in the work are made up of these same shapes. They march across the canvas in time to imagined music. We experience the feeling of movement, as we see the turning wheels catch and reflect the light while the gun is pulled past the viewer.

There are many ways of celebrating the end of war. Imagine that you are in a gigantic square in front of a Mayan Temple in Guatemala before the time of Columbus. It is crowded with people. We hear the beating of drums, but another sound comes from the sky. We look up and see a flock of eagles soaring above. On the ground are men in costumes made of bird feathers. They look like giant birds. Their huge bird helmets are fashioned with open beaks which seem to swallow the man. These bird-men swoop and bend to imitate the flight of the eagles. They are the *Eagle Warriors,* who celebrate their victory by entertaining a captive chief before they sacrifice him. This small figure is a whistle in the image of an *Eagle Warrior.* Compare the Etruscan warrior and this Guatemalan soldier. Which one looks to be better equipped for battle?

Eagle Warrior (7th to 10th century), Guatemalan;
The University Museum of the University of Pennsylvania.

Imprisonment was not always the fate of captives. Sometimes they were sold into slavery, killed, or offered as a sacrifice. Sacrifices had a religious nature, primitive people believing that the blood of one person would be a charm against the death of many.

Special utensils were made to conduct sacrificial rituals, such as this silver cauldron, which is about two feet in diameter and 16 inches deep. The meanings of the ancient Danish figures on the bowl have been lost to us, but the function of the bowl is thought to be that of a drowning vessel. A victim's head was held in the water until he died. It was a common practice in ancient civilizations to treat prisoners of war without mercy. Perhaps Winslow Homer's prisoners seemed so uncaring because they knew they would not be tortured and killed.

Gundestrup Caldron (about 400 B.C.), Celtic; National Museum, Copenhagen.

The Warrior's Games

After victory, what? Men who were trained as warriors found the periods of peace hard to fill. They loved the excitement of battle and the contest of man against man. The warriors known as knights were bound by oath to serve their king in times of trouble and to travel throughout the lawless lands of Medieval Europe protecting those in need of aid. When times were peaceful they traveled from country to country challenging other knights to compete in tournaments which tested the courage and skill of the participants. These tournaments were an important part of the social life of Medieval Europe and were as much a part of the festivities of the king's court, or noble's life, as were lavish banquets, feasts and pageants. In the tournaments the warriors found the kind of excitement and challenge experienced on the battlefield, but without loss of life and limb.

Tournaments were colorful spectacles. Knights from every part of the kingdom would gather for these contests. The joust

The Art of Jousting and Tilting by Leonard Beck (1480-1542); The Cleveland Museum of Art, Dudley P. Allen Fund.

was one of the games. Two armoured knights on horseback would charge at one another, each trying to knock the other off his horse. The unhorsed rider was the loser in the contest, as he would have been in battle.

Just as warriors were trained for battle, so young nobles were schooled in the art of jousting or tilting. The skill developed on the tilting field would later serve in time of war. The Emperor Maximilian I whom we have already seen on page 15 , commissioned the artist Leonard Beck to make illustrations for a picture book based on the emperor's life. This book, called the *White King,* was illustrated with woodcuts, some of which show the ruler jousting. Maximilian is seen in the foreground in this illustration, as he breaks his

opponent's lance, forcing the horse and rider to the ground. In the upper ground of the picture, two riders separated by a fence joust in the same manner, but the barrier eliminates the danger of the blindfolded horses either trampling, or crashing into each other. The speed and strength required in jousting is evident as the knights charge. We can see how the action would be exciting and dangerous.

In Conrad Marca-Relli's *The Joust,* there is clattering, banging action where dark shapes collide with white shapes causing an explosion of color. He tries to capture the impact of two bodies crashing into each other. Some of the shapes resemble shields or helmets, scattered by the force of the collision.

The Joust (1959) by Conrad Marca-Relli; Walker Art Center, Minneapolis.

The Combat of the Infantry from The War of Love by Jacques Callot (1592-1635); National Gallery of Art, Washington, D. C., Baumfeld Collection.

This is not a real battle. People stand watching without fear of being hurt. This is a drawing of *The War of Love,* part of a battle pageant staged for the entertainment of the de 'Medicis, a wealthy and powerful Italian family, and their friends. These pageants were similar to musical productions, being very elaborately designed by artists and engineers. Jacques Callot served as an assistant to the pageant engineer for the de 'Medici productions.

As an artist, Callot found the activities of the nobility of little interest, but the common man fascinated him. The people in the foreground are musicians, peddlers, gatecrashers, and generally rowdy street people gathered to watch the pageant. The foreground events are in great contrast to the order in the arena. These events seem more life-like than the battle being staged with its tiny puppet-like people in neat ranks. The care with which Callot records the pageant made his drawings useful in teaching military men of his time and later.

Chess Set (1961) by George Ortman (1926-   ); Collection of Mr. and Mrs. Howard Wise, New York.

To end this look at war and warriors we come to a battlefield where there are soldiers, commanders, kings, victors and losers and much movement, but no bloodshed—the field of the chessboard.

The ancient game of chess was known to the Chinese as early as the second century BC. It is a game of strategy, where one army faces the other on a battlefield of red and black squares, fighting a war to capture the enemy king. The pieces in the original game were the keys to waging war in that time: the king, the counselor, the cavalry, and the foot soldier. In times of peace chess was a means to exercise the mind in play battles. This is the most peaceful of the warrior's games, played without danger, and where only the player's skill, not his strength, counted.

Chess sets were made from precious materials of all types and craftsmen tried to outdo each other in originality of design. The challenge

of redesigning the pieces of this ancient game also interests today's artists. George Ortman, an American, designed this chess set carved from wood and painted in silver with red and yellow accents.

The traditional figures of king, queen, bishop, knight, castle and pawn, are no longer recognizable human figures, as seen on most chess sets. Ortman has selected forms alone to symbolize each of the pieces. The diamond is the king. The circle, an ancient sign for woman, is the queen. The cross, a sign for the Church, is the bishop. The heart is the knight, for knights should possess the quality of courage or heart. The square, the shape of many buildings, is the castle. The arrow is the pawn and indicates the direction of movement of this piece. Ortman has used a type of sign language which, when once explained, is not so far removed from the language we encounter every day in observing street signs.